LESSONS OF THE DEAD

BRETT ORTLER

Fomite
Burlington, VT

The poems listed below were first published in the following venues; their editors and publishers have my lasting thanks.

"What the Dead Tell Us About a Chicken with Its Head Cut Off"
— *Atticus Review*

"What the Dead Tell Us About the Road Back to the Living"
— *THE LAKE*

"What the Dead Tell Us About the Other World," "At Orientation," The Museum of the Lost"
— *Revolver*

"Adam and Eve See the First Tornado"
— *Permafrost*

"What The Dead Tell Us About Charon, The Ferryman of the Dead"
— *Rattle*

"What the Dead Tell Us About Heaven and Hell"
— *Lake Effect*

"What the Dead Tell Us about Gambling, Bookies, and Betting in the Afterlife"
— *Redactions*

"Cupid in Old Age"
— *Red Weather*

Copyright © 2019 Brett Ortler
Cover image: "Stella Painted Reflectively" sculpture by Barbara Zucker
All rights reserved. No part of this book may be reproduced in any form or by any means without the prior written consent, except in the case of brief quotations used in reviews and certain other noncommercial uses permitted by copyright law.

ISBN-13: 978-1-944388-84-3
Library of Congress Control Number: 2018967668
Fomite
58 Peru Street
Burlington, VT 05401

Contents

What the Dead Tell Us About the Other World	1
At Orientation	2
What the Dead Do When They Come Back	4
Adam and Eve See the First Tornado	5
What the Dead Tell Us About Fortune Tellers, Psychics, and Mediums	6
What the Dead Tell Us About the Road Back to the Living	8
What the Dead Tell Us About February 2nd	10
What the Dead Do On Halloween	12
What the Dead Tell Us About the Expulsion from Paradise	14
What the Dead Tell Us About Old Age, Retirement, and Migration	16
What the Dead Tell Us About Those Who Come Back to Life	18
What the Dead Tell Us About Heaven and Hell	19
The City of the Lost	20
The Museum of the Lost	21
What the Dead Tell Us About Death Himself	23
What the Dead Tell Us About Hell	24
What the Dead Tell Us About Charon, Ferryman of the Dead	26
What the Dead Tell Us About Gambling, Bookies, and Betting in the Afterlife	28
When Lazarus Was Brought Back From the Dead for the Second Time	29
What the Dead Tell Us About Temptation	30
What the Dead Tell Us About War	32
What the Dead Tell Us About Magic	33
What the Dead Tell Us About the Other Side of the Tunnel	34
What the Dead Tell Us About Death and the Dunk Tank	36
What the Dead Tell Us About the *Edmund Fitzgerald*	38
What the Dead Tell Us About Transportation	39
What the Dead Tell Us About Deep Time	41
What the Dead Tell Us About the Last Voyage of Henry Hudson	42
What the Dead Tell Us About Cupid in Old Age	43
What the Dead Tell Us About the Old Gods	44
What the Dead Tell Us About a Chicken With Its Head Cut Off	46

What the Dead Tell Us About Mycology	47
What the Dead Tell Us About the Mayor of the Dead	48
What the Dead Tell Us About Exoplanets and the Problem of Evil	50
What the Dead Tell Us About the *Titanic*	51
What the Dead Tell Us About Dead Children Washing onto Beaches	52
What the Dead Tell Us About Mount St. Helen's	53
What the Dead Tell Us About Paul Bunyan	54
What the Dead Tell Us About the *Weihnachtsfrieden*	55
What the Dead Tell Us About Mortsafes	56
What the Dead Tell Us About Congenital Analgesia	58
What the Dead Tell Us About Anatomy Murder	59
What the Dead Tell Us About Shadow	61
What the Dead Tell Us About the *Pater Familias* and the Last Breath	62
What the Dead Tell Us About Playing Dead	63
What the Dead Tell Us About Good Friday	64
What the Dead Tell Us About the Milky Way	65
What the Dead Tell Us About Multitasking	66
What the Dead Tell Us About the Lake Country	68
What the Dead Tell Us About The Number of People Who Have Ever Lived	69
What the Dead Tell Us About the Handbook to Heaven	70
What the Dead Tell Us About Andromeda's Wedding	71
What the Dead Tell Us About Lighthouses	72
What the Dead Tell Us About the Path of Totality	73
What the Dead Tell Us About Mourning	74
What the Dead Tell Us About Special Deliveries	75

For Kayli, Oliver, and Violet

Ach, Liebste, lass uns eilen,   Oh darling, let us hurry,
Wir haben Zeit   we have time.

—Martin Opitz

What you are now we used to be;
what we are now you will be.

—placard at the Capuchin Crypt

What the Dead Tell Us About the Other World

The surprise is
there's no surprise, no lake of fire or pearly gates,
just Death, the ticket-taker,
at the door, the entrance to the afterlife
blocked off by frayed velvet rope.
Death tears your ticket, and then resumes reading
his mystery novels—he can't get enough of them.
In life, he knows when you will die, and how,
but in fiction he doesn't have a clue, and he's surprisingly bad
at guessing. Inside, the afterlife is a waiting room—
you take a number, play Parcheesi, page through old newspapers
and *National Geographics*. It's not hell, exactly, but certainly not heaven.
Food is abundant, but strictly utilitarian, enough to get by,
bread and lukewarm water, Meals Ready to Eat, sardines.
And when they call your number, no one hesitates to go back,
not even if their past life was torture, violence, disease.
Everyone knows this is a carnival
prone to disaster, the hall of mirrors smashed by a blackshirt carnie,
kids choking on tainted taffy, but this is also the only place
for roller coasters, for fun, the only place you can carry
your newly won goldfish home in a plastic bag
though you know it will eventually die.

for T. Boss

At Orientation

They tell us we're lost,
but they hand out maps anyway
that clearly show us off to the side
with wild arrows pointing to the big question mark in the middle,
and we say, *Thanks, that's real helpful,*
and the stewardesses adjust their hats as they smile and say,
Oh, they're not for navigation, before shuffling us off towards the exits,
tiny doors, like tunnel entrances, just large enough to crawl through,
and give us tickets with exact times stamped on them,
like train tickets, but these come with props,
and each read *this is what you can expect,*
the man next to me had World War One printed on his, and they gave
him a helmet with a spike on top of it, and a single-shot rifle,
other people got all sorts of things, eye patches, wheelchairs, twin brothers
until everyone had an outfit—businessmen, fashion models, and farmers,
the soldier next to me looked at me
and said, *I don't like war,*
I don't even like action movies, before waving down a stewardess,
pushing the helmet into her arms, and saying, *I don't understand.*
And the stewardess smirked again, and said, *Don't worry, you won't,*
before checking her watch, and stepping out of the way
as the ticket-taker, sudden and imposing in a trench coat and fedora,
like he'd been in the SS in another life,
opened the soldier's door, and said, *I'll see you in 76 years, on the button.*
And the soldier crawled into his tunnel,
as did doctors, and plumbers, and teachers,
and others with outfits we couldn't make out or understand,
and we looked at each other before leaving, and smiled sheepishly.
At least we're dressed for the occasion, I said,
as the man in the trench coat

told me I had 82 years
as he opened the door
to some strange party.

What the Dead Do When They Come Back

They buy old photographs at thrift stores
for fifty cents, a dollar,
flipping through the piles
for a face they recognize,
anyone at all, the pictures yellow as an egg yolk.
Sometimes, they skim through the other items,
but most people don't leave much behind,
so the flapper rummages through vintage dresses
for a facsimile of the old style
and old men sift through garage sales
for old Spalding drivers or Louisville Sluggers.
Some find proof of their last life:
a flyboy downed in the Battle of Britain
traces the outline of his own name carved in granite
a professor opens a leather-bound volume
to find his name crossed out, another stamped above it.
Even Rameses II, peering in at his mummy,
doesn't recognize his own body,
that red hair, until he reads the placard. Even then,
he is astonished at how little is left
and what proof there is
of all those lost mornings and evenings.

Adam and Eve See the First Tornado

and think they are forgiven. They see it
from a distance, wound down
in a slender spiral
from a cloud the size of heaven.
They run toward it,
as if it were an angel come to them,
because they know only the basic burdens
of the earth: hunger, fear, and guilt
and because they recognize something
in the weather just before it touches down,
how it is calm, almost serene,
with a golden-green light
that reminds them of the Garden.
Only when they are close enough
to feel the rock and dirt flung against their skin,
and see trees torn from earth,
as if they, too, were being punished,
do they understand and retreat.
When the light returns,
they find their small, humbled house,
with its hail-stung garden
and all the downed trees
surrounded by ruined fruit.

for Chris

What the Dead Tell Us About Fortune Tellers, Psychics, and Mediums

They try to contact us, too
but you'd think they'd have more success,
given they have Ihmotep, Dr. Faustus, Aleister Crowley,
but after a few centuries of grand predictions that don't pan out,
the excitement wears off
and pretty soon the psychics and palm readers
find themselves making pancakes, and fortune tellers become bank tellers
or are telling passengers to please pick up the white courtesy phone
over the loudspeaker at the station.

There, like here, the basic physics are the same—
communicating across a great distance requires great power.
Even if a message gets through, what's left doesn't make much sense.
For example, in 1989, a child of six prays
to tell his grandfather, just gone from cancer, that he loves him.

Twenty years later
the grandfather gets a love letter
from Abelard to Heloise.
Dead already for two decades, he knows
there is no hotline to heaven
so he responds by reciting his grandson's favorite fable,
but by the time the message gets here
the child is twenty eight
and instead of a fox and grapes,
he dreams about a sultry redhead
who happens to be a vintner.

Undeterred, each night the old man tries again.

None of the messages come through entirely,
but each is its own strange gift, even the nightmares.
In one, the grandson finds a hydrogen bomb
covering most of his stove. Oblivious, he makes popcorn
and when he lights the remaining burner,
it whooshes to life, each flame like an individual wave
in a child's drawing of the ocean.

The grandson thinks nothing of the weapon of mass destruction
protruding onto the countertop
until the corn begins to pop, each kernel bursting like a tiny test shot
on a Pacific atoll. Then he begins to panic
and realizes that he has to warn his family,
his friends, everyone in the blast radius,
but it's too late, the countdown is nearly complete.

So he braces for the impending shock
but nothing happens
and he wakes up to find an empty stove
and a living room full of pets
free from any radioactive mutations.

He smiles a bit, then stops,
realizes that this was a dud, a delay,
just a precursor to the inexorable blast
and its sudden flood of light.

for M.E.V. and V.B.

What the Dead Tell Us About the Road Back to the Living

The truck stops make it manageable,
and the barkers selling bibelots from the great beyond—
inflatable scythes, maps to the homes of the recently deceased,
or the Programs! Programs! for the sideshows:
Sisyphus charging 10 bucks a pop then rolling his boulder uphill,
or Achilles throwing a right at Joe Louis
in a roadside ring.

But what's best is a cool booth for coffee and cake
and getting out of the worst traffic jam ever:
the seven-thousand year flood of us,
plus the Neanderthals, the chimps,
and the rest of the family tree,
everyone on a one-way street
to the only place worth going.

Those who try to stay behind
find Lot's wife, still a salt lick
and not much for conversation,
sad old Schopenhauer still contemplating suicide,
even after death. These are the ghost towns of the afterlife,
the dead-end dives with stale beer and bad music.

So it's all about hitting the road and edging ahead in line,
sneaking in front of the people from the Pliocene, none too bright,
or sprinting past a Stegosaurus distracted
by the family of dodos dawdling beneath its feet.

It takes a while,
but in between here and there, it's not all bad,

the sun and moon share the sky,
contrails crisscross like chalk marks
on a blackboard, and the sea,
with all ships sailing,
is a quilt of blue and white.

What the Dead Tell Us About February 2ⁿᵈ

Even minor holidays are important during long winters,
so the dead celebrate Groundhog's Day too.
Of course, there is no shortage of groundhogs in the afterlife,
but after a few millennia
a rodent pawing for its shadow
became less and less of a draw,
and the plain damn trouble
of spelling *Punxsutawney*
grated on everyone so much
they decided to liven things up by choosing
different forecasters.

Some choices were better than others.
The dodo was always the optimist—and always wrong—
but its slapstick grace endeared it to the crowds;
on February 2ⁿᵈ, you knew that it would tumble down
Gobbler's Knob no matter what.

Everyone knew that the selection of a juvenile velociraptor
was clearly a gimmick. It was uncooperative, to say the least,
and on a few occasions it escaped the night before
and there were reports of missing children.

At first glance, most of the living wouldn't recognize the holiday
as celebrated there. Here, it's custom to dress up—
the tailors of Punxsutawney will always have winter business—
but most of the dead dress down, no more corsets or tuxedoes.
Instead, they wear pajama bottoms and shirts that proclaim
they are the property of this-or-that athletic team.

Like us, they stand in the winter cold
and know that when the sun dawdles
just above the horizon for half the day
and it gets dark at half past four,
a spurious hope
is sometimes better than certain gloom.

    for Kayli

What the Dead Do On Halloween

On the day we pretend to be others
they try to remember.
At the family reunion over breakfast,
the father arrives early
and prepares the table—
there are steel plates and gussets,
Bowie knifes, teaspoons, and salad forks,

on the edge of the table
a vase overflows with enriched flour.
When the daughter shows up wearing a parka
and the son just a swimsuit and a snorkel,
the father simply grins and smiles
and shouts out what he can remember of the old language,
its hard consonants like the sound of dice thrown onto a wooden floor.

Finally, mother enters the room in a sombrero and an evening gown,
dancing *der Schuhplattler* before serving
a main course of lobster and French fries.
Then, all enjoy their juice boxes, and laugh and laugh
at their attempts to make toasts to one another:
To our maternal female!
To our familial resemblance!
To adhering together as an entity consisting of immediate family,
thereby retaining the original family parallelogram!

They laugh because they know
dying imposes a new mother tongue on everyone—forgetfulness—
and they have cheated it this long.
In a month, or maybe a year, the husband won't recognize

the wife's face in the newspaper, and the son will ignore his sister
busking for change at an intersection.

For now, they sing any songs they can remember:
Christmas carols, the alphabet,
even half-hearted attempts at the old national anthem,
the father proudly leads the family into "O Canada"
then stumbles after the second word. With a smile—
he shrugs and begins to hum along with the rest of the family,
the song's lyrics and tune as nebulous
as his wife's first name.

What the Dead Tell Us About the Expulsion from Paradise

The Book of Life was simple once
a blank scroll that a dutiful seraph amended
as God added to creation: the herb yielding seed,
great whales, Adam, then Eve
and all the creatures under their dominion.

The angelic scribe worried when Adam began assigning names.
Aloud, he congratulated him for the creativity
of *passenger pigeon* and *fly agaric,*
smiling as he added each name to the list,
but naming the flowers alone took fifty years.

Before Adam was created, naming the creatures
was the angel's only job,
but now, he realized how bad his names had been:
things with feathers, creatures that live where it is wet.

When they were finally finished, Adam smiled,
only to notice that the dinosaurs had been replaced with birds.
He shrugged, clapped the angel on the shoulder and said,
I guess we'll have to start over.

The seraph nearly shrieked.

A few hundred years later, just as they were
wrapping up revisions to their
eighty-seventh draft, Adam looked at a lichen
and began droning on about a new subspecies.

The angel had long since settled on his scheme,
and began rehearsing just
what he'd say to convince
the serpent.

What the Dead Tell Us About Old Age, Retirement, and Migration

Sanibel Island, Florida

It is a life of constant reminders.
Two dozen turkey vultures
circle over Sanibel Island,
each waiting for a specific person
to succumb to the ailment
or accident about to befall them,

and then there are entire cities with economies
that depend on the dying—
hearing aid commercials broadcast twice as loud as regular programming
funeral homes every few blocks,
and of course, the endless doctors and specialists,
the assisted-living homes and hospice care.

And the months are filled with expected tragedies,
solemn phone calls, memorials, funerals and end-of-life planning,
every obituary section filled with a familiar face
or two—next-door neighbors, tennis partners
or the woman down the street with emphysema,
who let her grandchildren of ten and six
drive her golf cart to get the mail
when they visited.

Even the birds seem like prophets—
in the fall, there are dozens of sudden arrivals—
orioles and bluebirds back from the north,
so many species trying to survive another season

by staying in the sun,

but in late winter there is a piecemeal departure
one, three, now half a dozen gone,
and each morning is quieter
and the trees are full
of less color.

What the Dead Tell Us About Those Who Come Back To Life

There is a tabloid culture there too,
and when Lazarus died for good,
the dead threw a welcome-back party,
and if you believe the stories some tell,
he was hopscotching between both worlds
as a parlor trick.

When he got back, everyone was there,
the celebrities, the paparazzi,
and the inevitable salesmen
who presented him with his own brands
of fake flowers, death palls, and funeral urns.

Everyone wanted to remember the old life
and crossing over. They asked him the same questions,
about the tunnel and the bright light.
It's not a train ride, he said,
and the world is the same sad place it always was;
but Lazarus was surprised to see the crowd
go quiet, and a woman sobbing softly
by the cocktail bar. He sighed and took a drink
from the table. *No, I'm sorry, I didn't mean it like that;
it's only sad because it's gone again,*

but I have one story you might like to hear.
And the crowd looked up and listened
as he told them how Christ had steadied him
with a hand on his shoulder after raising him from the tomb.

What the Dead Tell Us About Heaven and Hell

They explain it in stories.
In one, there is woman in a garden
of a ruined plantation where the bricks
of the main house burned
long ago, but the terraces are still tended,
and gardenias grow in groups
of three or four. And a man is with her, and he loves her.
But it begins to rain, the water is cold on their skin,
and in that moment he knows he will go north and lose her.
For the first time in his life, he believes in heaven and hell,
not as far-flung countries, but as twin cities,
with skylines in plain sight of one another,
both borders lined with billboards and bright lights,
and he realizes how hard it is to hear the difference
between a city full of worship and one full of wailing
and how easy it is travel
from one to the other.

for Sara

The City of the Lost

When you are absolutely nowhere
you're getting close.
Follow the trail of lost keys,
tour the lost homes
destroyed by flood or fire, all abandoned
but pristine; then go farther.
Dresden is here. Hiroshima. Nagasaki.
Visit the library of Alexandria;
go to the harbor where the *Lusitania* and *Titanic* sway
with lost wind and water.

At the park, the gods
picnic together; on blankets and green grass,
they eat forgotten fruit.
Overhead, Amelia Earhart
banks and whirls
in her Lockheed Electra.

From above, she sees all the lost lives, small
but sharp as starlight,
lives spread out farther than the sky.
In the distance, the dust rises,
and one can see a single-file line
leading from the known world
to another.

The Museum of the Lost

The tour guide is an orphan child
who leads a handful of sightseers and lookers-on
through the slanting stacks and wild piles of everything imaginable.
Like a bee to a favored flower,
she flits to one exhibit, then the next.
First she hovers over a lost portrait
by da Vinci and halfway through her history of the piece,
the painting disappears behind her back—
the staid subject's face fading first, then the background
and finally, the heavy frame,
first the gilding gone, then the cracking poplar beneath.

With a wave of her hand
she explains that this should be expected: Not everything is lost forever.
As if to prove her point, a rediscovered Rolex
worms its way out of a slumping pile of wristwatches
as a handful of forgotten hand-me-downs scatters across the top.

The next exhibit is no different—a wall full of fishing lures
glints in the distance, and as the group approaches,
a perch with three treble hooks twists free
and wings away. It was snagged ten feet up a tree,
found by a fisherman in Missouri, she says,
as she leads them to the next room, full of boats,
diesel-powered trawlers next to Greek galleys
and long-sunk German submarines with great gashes in the hulls.
Then a room full of the fishermen and sailors
themselves, lobstermen and whalers
next to pirates still showing signs of scurvy.

While the tour guides wend from one spot to the next,
the curators try to retain order. They scurry from room to room,
replacing placards, dusting displays, scratching out the old signage,
while workers paint new lettering,
but there's no way to remove all of the promotions
for the Pompeii exhibit, which were carved into stone
and no hiding the impression
the *Titanic's* hull left on the courtyard floor,
or the 900 feet of nothing
where she once stood.

When the great ship disappeared,
the curators dashed around
like doctors after an epidemic,
speaking with the visitors
perhaps only to break the silence
and to account
for all the suddenly empty rooms.

What the Dead Tell Us About Death Himself

The flowers he purchased
on the day of your birth
are still clutched in one hand,

and all the other gifts he planned to give you
over the years are next to him:
a Skeletor toy for when you were five,
a puppy, long since dead; a turtle, dead;
a goldfish, dead, the bowl last held water
when you were in the sixth grade.

On the table in front of him, beside all the empty cartons of cigarettes,
is a list of every time you have stood him up,
all the near misses:
the telephone pole you wrapped your car around after dozing off
after a shift at the outlet mall,
the 'flu' you shook off in college that was really meningitis

and the thousands of planned "appointments"
where you never showed:
the train you missed that crashed,
the dinners where you chose fish or a vegetarian option
instead of the tainted beef
or the extra spicy wings you would have choked on.

Now he finally has you
but says nothing, thrusting the mummified bouquet
into your hands before marching
you the length of the corridor
and throwing open the door.

What the Dead Tell Us About Hell

After a thousand years,
the desperate shrieks of the damned
no longer echoed off the black basalt walls
as often as when the torment was fresh,
and after five thousand years,
the cries from the lake of fire
were half-hearted, and then outright phony
but the demons overseeing perdition never noticed
because the boss was off on business
and Beelzebub and friends were too busy
leaning on their pitchforks and telling dirty jokes,
stopping only to snatch a cinder from an updraft
to light a cigar.

When Satan finally stopped in,
the first thing he saw
was a sinner securing a volleyball net
by bashing a stake with brimstone.
He knew there was real trouble
when he saw the tiki torches and their gentle wisps of flame
instead of the guttering oil lamps, each glint of light
as sudden as a thrust from a harpoon.

Perdition had become a party—
everyone knew the lake of fire had fish,
and charred charter boats skimmed across the surface,
while half of hell parasailed on the updrafts.

Satan knew he had to change locations and vary the punishments,
so now the venue varies every few weeks

more often than not, hell is on earth—
Europe during the Black Death,
Cambodia under Pol Pot, pretty much anywhere in Nebraska.
Out of a given millennium, the original hell is vacant 990 years
of the time and a tourist attraction for the blessed.

Planning all this takes time,
so Satan holds meetings in hotel conference rooms
under the dull glow of PowerPoint presentations;
every so often a couple minions doze off, wake up suddenly
and lean into the light. For a moment
a pair of plastic nametags block the projector beam
and shine as bright as the morning star:
Hello, my name is Mammon. *Hello, my name is* Asmodeus.

Never a fan of interruptions,
Satan sets the conference table on fire.
His minions rush to fan the flames—to flatter him—
this triggers the fire alarm and the emergency sprinklers,
shorting out the laptop with all the infernal plans.

The other demons disappear at once
when they know they have to start again.
Undaunted, Satan eventually skulks
into the lobby, cutting in line for coffee
at the continental breakfast.

Still half-wet, he heads back to his room,
the honeymoon suite, where his daily stack of newspapers awaits.
He reads them all, seeking out the worst people
and stories he can find,
and it never surprises him
how easy Earth makes it to reinvent hell.

What the Dead Tell Us About Charon, Ferryman of the Dead

Charon is in a hurry, if you can imagine it,
revving the engine of his outboard motor with one hand
and pulling passengers in with the other,
the boat leaning toward water and righting itself
as each steps in and is guided to a seat—
or what passes for one on his ferry:
a lunch cooler, a tackle box, the lap of a larger neighbor—
and then the boat lurches away from the dock,
black smoke rising from the old engine,
the bow cutting through whitecaps.

Then, the sudden stop, the engine silent, the waves
steady against the hull, and the dead,
looking away from the final shore for the first time,
see Charon dressed like a lobsterman, his poncho bright as a banana,
with a fishing rod in hand, casting and reeling as fast as he can
because he's timed the journey there and back,
and knows he only gets a few casts per trip.

And with each cast, he swears under his breath, cursing the dead,
because there are always more to take,
because they keep him from fishing
because they made him into a tourist trap instead of a fisherman,
despite the dozen bridges across the Acheron,
the helicopters, the kayak and canoe rentals,
and every passenger reminds him of the first,
a young Abel with a knife in his back, trying to swim across
the wide water. When he first noticed Abel,
Charon was fishing and had a bass on the line

near the lilies. He cut his line to help the young man reach the shore.

Abel was quiet at first and winced when he saw a heron
spear a perch in the water. He sighed before speaking,
then told Charon what to expect, how things had changed,
Now there is suffering on earth, and everywhere in between.

What the Dead Tell Us About Gambling, Bookies, and Betting in the Afterlife

If we could take a look at the secret books, the folded-over files of the other world, we'd see what we're up against. The bets placed against every life. Any bookie will tell you I should have been dead twenty five years ago and two hundred times since. The obituaries are already written and the reporters have them ready, hanging in their hands. In those hypothetical headlines, the players are foreign and familiar: lightning, bad brake lines on a mountain pass, pills, peanuts. Diseases we've never heard of or diseases we know too well.

But that's not what they're betting on. For them, death is a short film, the previews, a chance for candy before the feature. The real show is rebirth. When one of the leading lights, Houdini, say, is brought back and starts his long walk down the red carpet, the betting begins—the bookies bark out the odds, two-to-one he comes back as a human, a thousand to one he comes back as a lamp. Then they place their bets and the crowds bend over the balconies and stand on their seats, they pump quarters into the tourist telescopes as the results are called off over the loudspeakers.

The house wins most of the time: Houdini, reborn, dies as an infant in Africa, but every once in a while a long shot comes through, good prevails, or a man and woman fall in love hard, fast and certain and a cheer goes up, the winners scribble on their scorecards, and the dead buy each other drinks and place more bets on things that should happen, but probably won't.

When Lazarus Was Brought Back From the Dead for the Second Time

His first thought was Jesus has gotta be joking
but this time Jesus wasn't there,
and neither were Martha or Mary.

Lazarus had planned for this.
But the hemlock he instructed his surviving family
to pack into his pall was gone,
so he stood and stretched
and stumbled into light
a second time.

But his clothes had rotted,
so he walked down the streets
of the West Bank nearly naked,
with a sword, which was to do the trick in last resort,
crumbled to the hilt and hanging from his hands.

He tried to speak with those he saw
but didn't understand the Arabic or even the Hebrew
he heard. He was only half-listening, anyway;

he couldn't stop staring at the starlight of the city of David
in the distance, the lights on each street burning
like belief once had in his chest.

The police came quickly, taking him for mentally ill.
On the ride to the station, he looked out the window and up—
the stars were dimmer than he remembered
and heaven farther away
than ever.

What the Dead Tell Us About Temptation

In the factories the workers fear contamination
more than anything else, so they take precautions—
at the lingerie workshop, the seamstresses dress as staid
as schoolmarms; on their lunch break, they sip Shirley Temples
and play pinochle in plain black dresses, bonnets and bifocals
that most don't actually need.
They scoff and snigger as the floor boss tells the new hire
about the time a newcomer arrived for an interview
in a patterned dress
and half the room races to the punch line:
Alas, the strumpet did not get the job!

Occasionally, a seraphim sweeps down
to give a speech thanking them for their difficult, necessary work,
and noting that *all of the souls in perdition and purgatory
are, well, too occupied to make their own sinful apparel.*
As always, he leaves to wild applause.

But eventually, a Prudence or a Trudy or a Chastity
sees one too many corsets and pushups
and eventually sneaks off to slide on some satin leggings
and later, a friend helps her squeeze into a corset.

When the laces are wrenched
tight for the first time, the pain in her ribs
is as sharp as a spear
so she shimmies out of it
and back into her work clothes.
But the next day, walking home,
she notices the telltale curve of a flattering bra

on more than one passerby,
and a seraph leaps into the air,
the wind catching his tunic enough to betray
the muscle shirt beneath,

and she knows
even heaven is home to a black market
and almost everyone is buying
something.

What the Dead Tell Us About War

The trade doesn't seem quite fair: a frayed ribbon
and a piece of bronze with *The Great War for Civilization*
pressed into it in exchange for all that shrapnel.
At the least, parity seems fair: one medal awarded
for each piece of metal still inside.

Of course we'd need so many medals
that we'd run out of money for war,
but you wouldn't care if you could see
every army shimmering in the sun,
each Medal of Honor recipient brighter
than the mirror of Perseus,
and then the coffins
coated in bronze, purple, silver,
each held aloft by the survivors
and glowing like golden boats.

And behind this forward guard,
the undecorated masses—
the disappeared, the collateral, the kids,
all marching forward, forward,
finally ready to reckon,
to tabulate, to make clear
each war's final toll.

What the Dead Tell Us About Magic

Loss is the only trick
he knows. The posters
make that clear enough:
I make things disappear.
Shows around the clock.

The show's always the same:
he calls another unwilling volunteer,
forces them down into the chair,
and *voila*, there's the snap of his velvet cloak,
a flick of his wand, Canada yew,
and a quick grin at the empty seat.

He never explains the trick,
but expects applause, getting none.
Jilted, he calls up someone else:
a bystander, or your mother or my mother.

His trick cards long forgotten,
dusty and splayed out across the floor,
the show repeats again and again,
and eventually even he can't stop it.

Meanwhile, the rabbit molders,
looking on from its top hat tomb.

What the Dead Tell Us About the Other Side of the Tunnel

The first thing you see is a doctor trying to kill you.
If your eyes happen to flutter open, he'll put a hand
on your shoulder and say *I won't let anything happen to you*
before plunging a syringe into your chest.

If this doesn't work, the trauma team barks out vital signs
and the doctor orders every conceivable countermeasure
to what's happening on the other side.

One side gives norepinephrine to raise blood pressure,
the other, nitroglycerine,
the tit-for-tat can go on for days.

When things get desperate a nurse breaks out the belladonna
or strychnine or an orderly commandeers the crash cart
and rams it again and again against the operating table.

This is technically against the rules
but given the quotas and the overtime, it's overlooked;
sometimes a sudden crash
is enough to jar someone out of the old life.

When the heartbeat finally stops,
there is no applause. Like here the doctors file a few papers,
maybe shake hands then walk away.
Death is the first routine,
but coming to
is always new. There is no analog
for losing everything,

waking up alone and naked
on a metal table
under a new and glaring light.

What the Dead Tell Us About Death and the Dunk Tank

Eventually, a tattered baseball
carves through the twilight
and caroms off the target,
dropping Death into the dark water
shipped straight from the Lethe.

Everyone wants their chance
at even this paltry payback
so the other attractions are almost abandoned: Lazarus, unsmiling,
not because of the sinners lamenting in hell, as legend tells it,
but the indignity of having to offer himself up for autographs
and selfies in order to have a chance at making a sale of his Miracle Diet.

And then there is Christ, starting the music
on the stereo at the cakewalk, then sneaking away
for a few moves in the simultaneous chess game
against the Princes of Hell one booth over.
When the music stops, he materializes
in the middle of the cakewalk, shrouded in fire and light,
exclaiming *I have returned again to judge the living and the…*
before snuffing out the flames with a flick of his hand and shouting
Just kidding, everyone wins a cake!
This secret long since out, everyone shares cake
while they wait their turn for the dunk tank.

Death thinks the game is rigged, but the cold water
of the Lethe makes him forget each time.
Arms crossed, he smirks as each ball ricochets
off the backdrop or sails past the mark,
so when one strikes the target,

he's totally unprepared
for the icy water, the jeers from the crowd,
and the shock of the sudden drop.

What the Dead Tell Us About the *Edmund Fitzgerald*

> *"We are holding our own."*—the last transmission from Captain Ernest McSorley

It's true for a moment, or a week,
or a decade, then the radiologist finds a mass,
gray and grainy as a photo of a moon rock
or a friend starts forgetting,
first the little things, movie plots, appointments,
but soon she can't remember her favorite movie
or slip loose of her seatbelt. Eventually, she doesn't remember
her children, her husband, her own face in the mirror.
Living like this must be like trying to read
from a burning book—the lucid moments
are a page or two, but the paper is already browning
around the edges and words are falling into ash
as fast as you can read them.

Now imagine that's your wife:
standing fast with the water sweeping over the rails,
the ship listing, both radars gone,
the great black wave approaching
and the only way to go is down.

for Joyce

What the Dead Tell Us About Transportation

You start with a bare sledge
among the sastrugi and the fog
but it breaks and you see a Norwegian flag,
and then the Union Jack, a tent and Lawrence Oates
with the primus stove burning
even though the weather is balmy.

Without a word, he thrusts a cup of hot tea
into your hands, then sweeps aside the canvas flap
and steps out, saying *I am just going outside and may be some time,*
before popping back in immediately, guffawing.
His running gag complete,
he gives you a map—blank—
a pouch of Deutsche Marks,
and when you ask where you should go next,
he dutifully recites his lines, and points at the
slapdash X that marks the South Pole:
That's as far you can get, nowhere to go but north.

So you sledge and sledge
until you find Scott's Hut or if you're lucky, Shackleton's
and you wedge the whiskey from the floorboards,
before a ship arrives
and takes you away to
Elephant Island, then South Georgia,
all the waypoints on the way to civilization,
though not the one you were expecting:
the Sumerians, then the ancient Egyptians, the Mycenaeans.

Most give up the search for their old life
even though the afterlife is the first boomtown,

and the arrival of its assembly line of blight: sunken ships,
boarded-up houses, tainted brownfields.

Others leave, and find a new Northwest Passage,
or save up enough for a seat on a passenger train
pulled by a steam locomotive
only for the conductor to announce that the crew has just learned
the tunnel ahead dead-ends in dolomite.

So the train stops, and everyone aboard
clambers out and down to the tracks
to start again and find another way.

Eventually, almost everyone gives up,
but for a few everything else becomes irrelevant
and they try again and again
working their way up
from barefoot or a bare sledge
to a galley, then a caravel, eventually,
a Wright Flyer, a DC-3,
each vehicle one step closer to the present.

No one knows if anyone's made it;
the radios return only static,
and the telegraphs have all been
silent since the last cryptic message was received:

Rosabelle, Believe,
Rosabelle, Believe,
Rosabelle, Believe.

    for EW

What the Dead Tell Us About Deep Time

Wide and deep, its basin cut
from the Precambrian,
it is the first public pool.

All deep end, there is no way to touch bottom
or to escape, so everyone struggles to stay afloat
and fights for any advantage: water wings, kickboards,
pushing a struggling neighbor underwater.

The lifeguard is Death himself,
and he occasionally makes a small show of assistance: saving the whales
or the California Condor,
but everyone remembers the Great Dying,
one species after another forced from the high dive,
the froth from the struggle at the surface, then silence,
except for the jangling of the leg irons
and the endless columns of bubbles
rising in the dark water.

What the Dead Tell Us About the Last Voyage of Henry Hudson

Setting Hudson and his loyal crew adrift
was bad enough, but the mutineers forced his boy, maybe fifteen,
into an open boat, and the sick crewmembers, too.

When the frantic paddling ceased
and the *Discovery* was finally out of reach,
they had to have known they were finished.
No supplies, a hundred miles north of treeline;
maybe a few survived until autumn.

Let's not pretend that we are any different.
Each of us will be forced into an open boat, alone,
amid the blind leads and the pack ice.
Eventually, the only thing you can do is nothing,
except stare as the aurora stream across the sky,
the banners of heaven unfurling a welcome
for someone else in the distance.

What the Dead Tell Us About Cupid in Old Age

He's gone deaf and blind.

Just last week, they placed him here, at the Village at Delphi.
I told them it was Delphi, Indiana,
and a retirement community, not Greece,
but they didn't listen, and he's been shooting people with darts ever since.

Now we have widows necking in wheelchairs,
septuagenarians serenading,
(one woman fell in love with Alex Trebek after an arrow hit her TV).
Last week, I disrupted three games of strip bridge,
two candlelit Salisbury steak dinners,

and we had to replace half of the Craftmatic beds because of overuse.
Cupid is there for all of it, overweight and grinning like a fat baby,
hardly hovering, his tiny wings whirring like the engine of an old car.

I'm just a nurse, I can't handle this. I'd give anything for a Hercules or an
Odysseus. Instead, I've got Charlie,
an old Air Force pilot who pledges to defend my honor
and begins to chase after Cupid,
though Charlie is half out of his bathrobe and has forgotten his teeth.

for Emily

What the Dead Tell Us About the Old Gods

If they're lucky, belief lasts for five hundred years,
maybe a thousand. Then they become a blur of brushstrokes
in the background of a painting, a corporate logo
or the subject of an anthropology dissertation,
but they're only mentioned in the past tense,
so they take whatever work they can get.
Dionysus runs an international beverage firm
and manages a petting zoo in honor of long-dead Pan,
and when the scent of a barbecue
from the park a few blocks over
reaches Ceres atop
the Board of Trade building in Chicago,
she clambers down only after receiving a terse text
from Zeus—*rules are rules; barbecue qualifies as a ritual sacrifice*—
so she perfunctorily ensures that the harvest
of her patrons in Illinois will be bountiful
while those of their enemies—Iowa!—will not.

When they're really desperate, they end up shilling for local TV:
When Anu, God of Heaven,
needs to get around in southwest Florida,
I deign to visit Honest Ziggy's
where I know I will get a fair price.

A god's power depends on belief,
so they all take a seat in the great theater eventually,
sipping flat soda or failing to free the
last Raisinettes rattling along the bottom of the box
even though they can recall every moment
of their once unchecked power

and can't understand how the story
on the great screen
can hurtle forward without them.

What the Dead Tell Us About a Chicken With Its Head Cut Off

After the glint of the knife and the head pressed
into the heartwood of the oak
and its one hundred and fifty three rings,
there is a certain freedom to it. The blow itself is nothing—
anticipation's the real trouble, but once it is struck,
the legs kick loose, like springs snapping,
until every reserve is expended. The head, for the short time it survives,
is contemplative and relaxed. The mouth opens and closes,
quickly at first, then more slowly, a futile attempt to convey
everything it has just learned.
But it's the wings you need to watch out for:
they're out for revenge.
Like the claws, they will draw blood
amid their desperate scramble for heaven.

What the Dead Tell Us About Mycology

You're not *really* dead
until you sprout your first fungi.
Passersby are usually the first to notice,
and if they can tell you're new, they'll point it out,
and applaud, and others soon join in,

a host of strangers staring and congratulating you. When it happens
it doesn't take long for the street vendors to notice
and they veer toward you with everything needed
to document the find for posterity: wax paper, field guides,
the cheap chains for the keepsake necklaces
rattling as the pitchmen close in.

After the first, other forms of fungi follow,
as your body falls to pieces,
a full-fledged mushroom might form,
a ghoul fungus sprouting from a shoulder,
slime molds appearing on your shins,
but this becomes more a matter of hygiene
than outright decomposition,
and many opt to avoid plucking
or shaving them off. Instead, they culture them,
wearing special outfits to provide a substrate
for the luminescent species, so when the long twilight ends
and the pure dark returns each night,
the dead can gather together,
on an island of dim, but present, light.

What the Dead Tell Us About the Mayor of the Dead

The mayor of the dead is *so glad you've arrived*
and hands you the keys to the city,
then he greets the decedent behind you
and gives them a pair, which his attendants
unload from a line of overloaded wheelbarrows
that stretch beyond the horizon. The mayor's so busy
with the vagaries of the line—wars, epidemics, baby boomers—
that there's not time to explain. So the dead are born again
into a world they don't understand,
and they stumble from door to door
with a set of keys the size of garden shears.
Everywhere the billboards and placards
relay the same message:
I have prepared a house for you
but no one knows which one, exactly. Eventually someone tries
a lock and the door opens, and then everyone's turning keys,
behind one door there's a Neanderthal reading Spenser
behind another, one of the dogs who played Lassie and
the first Benji—real name, Higgins—
howling at a documentary about cats.

Occasionally, you discover more recent transplants:
a woman dead from bone cancer still mourning a husband and children,
or a family, lost in a car wreck, thrust into an unfamiliar world.
The dead grieve as much as we do.
Babies are born into a world of novelty,
but when a 58-year-old man leaves the only world he's ever known
and awakes to find a synonym of the life he's left behind,
you can understand the long nights of drinking
enveloped in the TV light, bottle caps found in couch cushions

days later like pocket change. There, like here, the long nights linger
into the afternoon, but there are no suicides
the second or third time around.
A total lack of a pattern, repeated
is pattern enough—after a lifetime or two
everyone figures out we're stuck in a randomized cycle of love
and wonder and generous helpings
of pain and terror and loss.
The point isn't to escape or understand
or even endure. This is what we have.
It is beautiful and boring and hard,
usually all at the same time.

What the Dead Tell Us About Exoplanets and the Problem of Evil

The old story about the ark isn't exactly true. He didn't wipe out everyone except Noah and his family because of unbelievers, but because creation was overwhelming. He expected that—thanks to omniscience—but expecting a disaster and living through it are different things, and we all do things we regret when stressed. Why else would you stamp a rainbow onto the sky when a handful of people were still thrashing on the surface?

On this planet, the old promise holds, at least for now, but things got out of hand elsewhere. There are 10^{24} stars in the universe; that's 25 zeroes. Each probably has at least one planet, and some have many more, so sometimes there are ten, maybe ten thousand species that need salvation. But rules are rules. So now there's no time to answer prayers; instead, Christ preaches, suffers and dies, then rises again to head to the next world. Every now and again, an asteroid hits it before He gets there, or its ozone layer is erased by a gamma ray burst. God knows this, of course, and Christ arrives anyway, weeping, and God makes another promise he knows that he'll never keep.

What the Dead Tell Us About the *Titanic*

When there is no chance of rescue
you stumble onto the boat deck alone.
Whether it was cancer, a car accident, or anaphylactic shock,
you arrive to depart. The lifeboats are already in the water,
the flares spent, the SOS signals sent
but imperceptible to the crew of the *Californian*, her wireless shut off.
In the two hours and forty minutes it takes *Titanic*
to sink, one of the newly dead appears on deck
about every two seconds.
By the time her propellers are in the air,
there are more than 5393 on board, more than double her capacity,
but that's beside the point says the Boatswain
as he hands you an index card with the water temperature,
the average survival time, and the estimated arrival of the *Carpathia*.
A few scramble to launch deck chairs overboard
or construct makeshift rafts, but most simply stare
at the stars rising on the surface of the sea, the ocean at their feet,
their waist, and the shock of the final deluge
and a glimpse of their own reflections,
lost amid the depths
of heaven mirrored on the water.

for Robert Ballard

What the Dead Tell Us About Dead Children Washing onto Beaches

What if heaven is empty, hell too,
and God, His power spent on the Creation,
is a spectator, and has to watch
everyone, from Cain and Abel
on up, age, wither, and die? Today
it must be worse than ever,
a world teeming with dying,
especially His favorites, the kids,
dead from diarrhea or cancer or drowning after bobbing along
the Mediterranean for a minute or two, until the shoes
are saturated and the sweaters take on enough water
to drag even a strong swimmer down.
Imagine if you were helpless, sentenced to survive forever,
forced to watch everything disappear.

What the Dead Tell Us About Mount St. Helen's

"There was no sound to it, not a sound. It was like a silent movie and we were all in it."—Krau Kilpatrick, USFW employee

It's fitting it happened in silence.
We expect cataclysm to announce itself
with lightning or lava fountains,
but we pretend we are important.
By the time we realize what has happened,
the sky is dark and maybe we catch a glimpse
of the tephra curling down the mountain,
the horizon collapsing to gray. Either way, it pulls us along
like the November wind dragging a few stray leaves.
The great dark cloud has other places to be.

What the Dead Tell Us About Paul Bunyan

The stories never mention
how much he enjoyed the red foxes shrieking
as they were flushed from cover,
or the porcupines, half-asleep, raining down
from branches like oversized pinecones.
Most of all, he loved to plunge the edge of his ax
through the soft fur of the leaf litter
after all the trees were felled. He swept it like a scythe,
scouring the earth to the bedrock
like his idols, the glaciers of the Wisconsinan.
Every so often, it struck a boulder of jasper or banded iron,
and the shock reverberated
like the cannons that had echoed across the prairies a decade or so before.
When Big Paul was finished,
he looked back and smiled at the great wastes
he had left behind,
the Dakota and Ojibwe mostly gone,
the elk, moose and wolves extirpated,
the stumps jutting out like gravestones.

What the Dead Tell Us About the *Weihnachtsfrieden*

It's easy to understand: for the first time in a week they aren't fighting,
and they remember how quickly time passes
when the five-nines aren't hitting every few dozen meters.
For once it's quiet enough to hear the birds,
which haven't given up on Ypres yet. It's only 1914.

After all the occasional terror, the soldiers are bored,
and who really wants to fight on Christmas?
Of course, they know the distance between opposing trenches
down to the footstep,
and for the major who brought along his soccer ball,
that hundred meters was a miracle.

Most who played that night were dead within a year,
and after the pall of the gas,
other such minor truces died too.

Still, there is no doubting the smiles amid the slide-tacklers
slipping through the fresh frost,
or the shout of surprise from the goalie after a shot
deflected off the makeshift woodwork was lost
in the maw of the trenches behind him.

for EN

What the Dead Tell Us About Mortsafes

> *The sea gave up the dead that were in it, and death and Hades gave up the dead that were in them, and each person was judged according to what they had done.* —Revelation 20:13

Even at the Resurrection, there are delays.
A dozen pharaohs wake up piled in a tomb,
their funerary equipment gone, their amulets pilfered
and in a traveling exhibit somewhere in New Jersey.

Meanwhile, Christ isn't having any better luck.
Everything starts off as planned:
the clarion calls, the host of heaven,
then a quick close-up on the Book of Life
but then a gust of wind comes up and the threadbare binding
gives way and the pages leap skyward
like so many renegade doves,
ruining another take of the shot
that's had the angels in the air
for twenty centuries.

Christ has rehearsed his lines since Calvary
and loses his temper again,
killing off another few species by accident—
the giant panda, the Sumatran rhino. Then he remembers
the hominids, four million years' worth,
most pre-vocal, and he thinks of the millennia it'll take
to convince them to come down from the trees,
and walk toward a blinding light,
and he storms off to his trailer
and the Judgment is delayed again.

But the Resurrection has already occurred.
No one remembers the few mortsafes still in service,
the sharp raps of bone against wrought iron,
or all the other people lost in between. No one notices
the empty chair at center of the set.
After all these years, only the word *director* is still legible
on what's left of the canvas fluttering in the wind.

    for Brian Hayden

What the Dead Tell Us About Congenital Analgesia

At first it seems like a blessing,
an infant, crawling toward a toy,
stumbles and her forehead vaults toward a leg of the coffee table.
Expecting the worst, you flinch, then relax when she starts laughing,
even though you felt the impact through the table,
saw the coffee mugs leap from their coasters.

Then you see the blood,
and the kid notices too, and laughs even harder,
pushing it around on the hardwood floor
like finger paint.

That's only part of the trouble—
if you don't feel pain, you never know hunger
and then the child's teeth start to come in,
the hands and the fingers mangled by accident.
Sometimes it gets so bad they remove the baby teeth entirely.
Even then, the afflicted rarely live to five.

The moral's clear enough: wherever we are, this ain't heaven.
Pain is the first lesson; we must suffer to survive.

What the Dead Tell Us About Anatomy Murder

Over there, the past is always present
so it's always where you were from, what you did,
and then the real topic of conversation: how you died.
Tragic deaths aren't any easier to understand
a decade or twenty after the fact,
so they garner sympathy, tears,
maybe even an in for a gig in the afterlife
where you won't have to do any work: mortician, obstetrician, lifeguard.
Preventable deaths, on the other hand, are an embarrassment;
wherever you go the bathrooms are crowded
with lifelong smokers dousing themselves in Febreeze,
former alcoholics applying primer, then foundation
to cover up the stain of jaundice.
And joggers, everywhere, joggers,
plodding past in sweatsuits,
and Sotheby's-style auctions for any exercise products at all: 25 million
for an exercise bike, tens of thousands for Shake Weights,
even Abs of Steel.

Some deaths grant you a sort of sainthood, but unlike that of the martyrs,
who knew what was coming, at least. No, everyone understands
the patron saints of misfortune, the galactically unlucky,
the husband out for a walk with his wife
killed by a fire hydrant
dislodged by a fender-bender
or the dozen or so victims of anatomy murder from 1828,
who were killed only to have their bodies
splayed open hours later

so students could learn the precise mechanics
behind do no harm.

for HH

What the Dead Tell Us About Shadow

It's every child's first toy.
Toddlers erupt in great squalls of laughter when they wave hello
and it waves goodbye;
if we're lucky, it stays that way, at least for a while.

Sometimes, shadows disappear too soon
along with the people who made them.
Then, it couldn't become clearer:
we're followed by absence all our lives.

Go ahead, hold your hand up against the light:
that's death, right there, sprawling across the floor.
Walk around the block
and it'll tag along with you.

Once you know it, there's no sense running.
Your shadow is as clear as the silhouette
of a Liberty ship before the blackouts on the coast.
Eventually, it slides into view of a periscope
hidden in the distance
and you catch an echo of the order
Torpedo los.

What the Dead Tell Us About the *Pater Familias* and the Last Breath

In terms of death rituals it's more awkward than most.
Dying is hard enough without tourists,
especially when it's the nephew you never really liked,
the chubby, selfish one who's only there because he knows
he'll get something out of the deal,
his jowls pressed against your face for the inheritance,
and then it happens—in your death throes—
with the kid hovering over you to take in your last breath,
you spasm, jump forward and French kiss him on accident.
There you are, dying, and your last sight on Earth is Brayden
recoiling at your accidental assault, and as the famed tunnel's
open aperture snaps to a focus, with the angelic choirs in the background
the only thing you notice is *That's disgusting*
and *I never liked him anyway.*

What the Dead Tell Us About Playing Dead

Most of the time St. Peter doesn't have to consult the Book of Life.
You have to be a real asshole to go hell, and getting a jolt—eternity—
is unheard of unless you're Höss, Tamerlane or Andrew Jackson.
The line to heaven is mostly kids,
always has been, so Peter does his best to distract them.
A few thousand years teach you a few tricks,
and now he's a master of pratfalls
and quick to bust out the balloon animals—which he invented—
but he spends most of his time explaining absence,
why dad and mom and grandma are missing
why no in line is sleepy or hungry.
It's been like this ever since Peter warmed himself by that fire.
He doesn't understand any of it:
the constant crush of children
pushing past toward heaven and its playgrounds,
the clothes he doesn't recognize or the languages he doesn't understand
or why he's standing there
where there are no gates at all.

What the Dead Tell Us About Good Friday

Weather rarely happens when you're watching.
The fish are biting, or the ducks are flying,
or your kid stops spelling *mom* in the dirt long enough to field a grounder
when you get the call. You answer, pause, find a way to say *OK*,
then hang up, forgetting to say goodbye.
The world dims as the sun is lost behind a squall.

What the Dead Tell Us About the Milky Way

Most of the people who have ever lived
are forgotten.
Now think of the stars.

What the Dead Tell Us About Multitasking

Death used to enjoy his work,
especially during the population bottlenecks
when he knew every person on Earth by name, all five thousand of them,
and he'd show up at their hearth with panache,
tearing down the hides that served as a front door
like the sheriff of a small town bearing a warrant,
before dragging away his quarry.

By the year 10,000 he knew he was in trouble:
managing a global population of four million
amid famines and plagues and the never-ending column
of expectant mothers, and often, their children.
Once the population hit the billions,
he needed all the help he could get—
malaria, then smallpox, polio,
now nicotine, opioids, and his other collection agents,
but it's never enough to keep up.

He weeps as the life expectancy Take a Number Sign
ticks up again in Monaco, where those bastards
are almost ninety on average,
and screams in his soundproof office at Phillip Morris
as worldwide deaths reach 151,600 a day,
almost two per second.

That's not counting the close calls,
the worst trouble of all—Near-Death Experiences.
For every death, there are X near misses: the heart stops,
the brain starts to die, and Death gets the call,
but when he arrives, the defibrillator does it work,

and the patient survives, at least for a few more minutes.
So he leaves for another call, another person he'd overlooked:
a woman who should have died in London
during the Blitz celebrating her 113th birthday,
and when he shows up mid-party
there's cake and a forest of candles, and the birthday girl giggling,
surrounded by a crowd of well-wishers born before Kitty Hawk.
And in the background, a TV report
about 80 is the new 60
given the latest clinical trials shown to reverse aging.

What the Dead Tell Us About the Lake Country

It's a perfect day, but the sun shines so much on the water
that it's hard to look at, a shimmering arrowhead of light,
so you look down, to the surface, the gradations of green
and the last flash of your copper lure before the grayish black,
and everyone reminiscences, talking funerals,
how diagnoses played out at first,
before anyone knew they'd turn fatal.

Later, off the water, someone looks up to see the stopped clock
on the wall, ten seconds shy of 4:02,
morning or evening no one remembers, and we move on.
Whether it's a mobile home park on a lake, or a suburb outside of Paris,
we're all crammed here together and we don't know why.
The only thing we really know is now,
the beauty of burning magnesium throwing light,
the child's wild smile as he traces out the letters of his name in smoke.
Then it happens—he disobeys the repeated command,
and there is weeping, then cool water and acetaminophen,
finally sleep, another memory
made of a first wound.

for Oliver

What the Dead Tell Us About The Number of People Who Have Ever Lived

There are 7.5 billion people alive on Earth; 107 billion people have ever lived.

For every person alive today, there are 15 of the dead, a number that is no coincidence, because a squad of 16—including you—is enough for starters, a solid bench and a few reserves for nearly every team sport in human history. Forget family, or friends, the first people you meet in death belong to your team; they've been watching you since birth analyzing your strengths, and weaknesses, slotting you into various lineups, and scribbling plays on clipboards. The famed white light isn't heaven: it's the halide lights of a football field—tryouts—for squash, jai-alai, Meso-American ball games, (sans the redundant ritual executions), any contest that fills the seats for a few years. But always baseball and soccer, the perfect games. In football and basketball, Goliath always wins, and a computer program can play 840 million chess games in 6 years; it'd take an average person a century, 5 games a day, to play just under 200,000. In some things, there's no catching up, but on a baseball diamond or a soccer pitch full of Neanderthals, Cro-Magnons, and peasants from the Tigris, the Indus, the Yangtze, and Five Points, or the occasional wild Gaul warrior streaking, literally, across the field, a millennia might as well be last Monday. For proof, consider the third base coach and managers assigned to each team, always archaic hominins, *Australopithecus*, *Ardipithecus*, pre-language. If you're lucky, you get *Homo Habilis*, capable of understanding hand signals, a few words, but always flailing with his arms wildly from third base in the direction of the hot dog vendor: *Man has meats, attack!* Or the soccer coach, a *Sahelanthropus tchadensis*, one of our oldest common ancestors with apes, not howling for once and instead staring at the dry-erase clipboard for most of the second half, tracing and retracing the outline of her own hand again and again.

What the Dead Tell Us About the Handbook to Heaven

Almost everyone takes a look at the preamble—all 75 volumes—shrugs their shoulders, and heads back to Purgatory, content with its rest stops and roadside sculptures. The World's Largest Prairie Chicken, the Largest Ball of Twine Rolled By One Person. In heaven, it's more than just *kosher* or *halal*: there's no singing, or laughing, and after the incident in Eden, no "children" under the age of 85, plus the volumes of phrases that are unpleasant or problematic, the subjects you should always avoid. Heaven's a dead place. God is somewhere, we suppose, locked away in a theater, watching *Ice Station Zebra*, or home videos of the Creation. If you want proof, take a chance by humming Hallelujah, or blaspheming: earth may quake, or it might not, the birds will call, but the sun will rise tomorrow and whatever end you find will be your own.

What the Dead Tell Us About Andromeda's Wedding

There was no giving-away ceremony. King Cepheus, squat as a rambler, stepped forward to take his daughter's hand, but she slapped him across the face with what was left of one of the monster's webbed feet. In the distance, Perseus waited at the edge of the cliff. Andromeda paused, brushing off tentacles and picking off the stray suckers still clinging to her arms and her neck. What Perseus hadn't slashed was still alive, despite Pegasus alighting over it, here, then there, before landing with his full weight, whinnying and snorting as it wailed and gurgled. Perseus watched, and laughed, so her parents did too.

Andromeda tried to look at him, but he kept turning the shield of Athena, so between the heat and the light, she could only trudge forward with her eyes closed. He had saved her, it was true, but she was a girl, and he was a man, and he saved her only after specific conditions. As she walked, the chain from a shackle trailed behind her, one that her mother had affixed so gently. Twenty feet away from Perseus, Andromeda looked back and saw the monster, its gills fanning out for water—sad, sorry, in need of saving—and she knew just what she had to do.

for Violet

What the Dead Tell Us About Lighthouses

Whether from the pilothouse of a ship offshore
or the museum inside the former keeper's house,
every one is a warning: Schooners may no longer split
upon the rocks here, but how many cars flipped
and foundered at Silver Cliff on 61
with Dylan playing on the radio
and a pie from Betty's in the back seat?
The warnings are all around us: foghorns, the monthly tornado sirens,
the diesel train's quick, short blasts to the kid wearing headphones
on the tracks, laughing and texting friends
about beer and summer break
despite the tremors beneath his feet
and the ditch lights from the engine
climbing up his back.

What the Dead Tell Us About the Path of Totality

Seen from heaven, you might not notice.
There's a blot on the Earth, sure, but it goes away.
Only in person is it an abyss.

Maybe you get the news just after the kid wakes up on a weekend,
and he buries himself in the bedspread, crying.
Or during lunch at work and you drive home, bleary eyed,
hummus and crackers still scattered across your desk.

That's when the birds go quiet,
and the sun goes dark, wreathed in fire. It appears again
on schedule for everyone else
but you have to begin orienteering, learning how to wayfind,
staring at the sky long enough
until you can make your own way back.

What the Dead Tell Us About Mourning

The last death you mourn
is your own, even if it was expected,
colon cancer, emphysema
or suicide, the lone casing found in your lap,
the handgun on the hardwood.
It's not that you weep for yourself;
you see your friends or family.
A daughter without a father
scrambling for money just to make the funeral,
hitching a ride to the service and arriving
to the scent of the flowers already dying.
Or you look over and witness how the phone call played out:
your son-in-law, answering, pausing,
his voice cutting out for long enough for the six-year-old
grandson to notice, spring up, and once the news was relayed, dash off
to bury himself amid the blankets of his bunk bed, wailing
for the better part of a summer. Loss is reciprocal,
and someone always regrets your passing
even if you don't realize it. When Abel realized
what had happened, he cradled the dagger in his hands
weeping for his parents, the first to lose a child,
two, if you count Cain. Abel wandered, like his brother,
until others began to arrive. Today, after the tumult of the operating room
or the slow fade of hospice, you find yourself circuiting
the clinics and empty halls of the hospital,
circling the cafeteria or simply standing
in front of the greeting card spinner
at the pharmacy, spinning it again and again
all the birthday and graduation slots empty,
the only card left reading
I wish you were here.

What the Dead Tell Us About Special Deliveries

The trucks are always driving, winding from street to street. They appear without notice—the drivers bounding up to the front step with the news, good or bad, no matter whether it's Christmas, summer break, or a week before a wedding. But there are a lot more trucks on the streets emblazoned with *Tragedy and Woe, Inc.* than with the sunnier competition. This world slants toward sorrow, maybe four to one. Sometimes deliveries arrive one after another, you see a child on an ultrasound and start planning, but it disappears after a few weeks.

After decades of this it's easy to understand why the Sumerians were fatalistic, expecting the floods to come at any time, or why Christians are convinced this place is a shadow of something pure. That's the only part about the Eden story that makes sense: this place could be perfect, but it isn't, so we are left with what we have: the long light of autumn, the sharp air after sunrise, looking down to admire the sharp yellow blooms of the mums, freshly planted after the wake.

This book would not have been possible without many people.

Marc Estrin and Donna Bister, for their work on this book, and for allowing me to become a Fomite author. It's an absolute honor, and I couldn't be more excited.

My parents, Dale and Mary: for their support, and more than anything, their love. My sister Emily deserves a special shout-out here too. Love ya, sis.

My wife, Kayli: My first reader and only love, she takes the time to hear every new poem, good or bad.

To Kathryn Nuernberger, one of the finest poets and essayists I know, for her generosity and incredibly kind words about the book.

The myriad of great teachers I've had the privilege to know: Mark Vinz, for introducing me to Bly, Bishop, and Edson and all the other poets who really made me want to write; Christopher Howell, for serving as my thesis advisor, his great poems, and crafting a reading list that I still refer to today; to Mark Bender, for those book spinners filled to the brim with Kurt Vonnegut and Orwell, and serving as the best possible English teacher a kid could want.

At Eastern Washington University: Jonathan Johnson, Sam Ligon, Gregory Spatz, Nance Van Winkle, and Wayne Kraft.

At Minnesota State University Moorhead and Concordia College: Laura Fasick, Gordon Jackson, Al Davis, Ken Bennett, Kevin Zepper, John Early, Jonathan Clark, and the whole crew at the MSUM Philosophy Department.

In the Minnesota poetry scene: Todd Boss, Tim Nolan, Joyce Sutphen, Jamie Haddox.

To my writerly pals who have read this manuscript before it was published: Jeffrey Morgan, Jeremy Halinen, Kimberly Lambright, and Eric Thomas Norris.

My thanks are also due to Shira Richman, William Childress, Sara Saylor, Adam O'Connor Rodriguez, Victoria Brockmeier, Michele Harmeling, and Blake Butler.

About the Author

Brett Ortler is a writer and an editor from the Twin Cities. His poems, essays, and articles appear in *Fatherly, Salon, Yahoo! Parents, HuffPost, Scary Mommy*, as well as in a variety of literary magazines and websites, including *The Nervous Breakdown, Fanzine, Revolver, Ascent,* and *Rattle*, among others. He is the author of nine books, most of them popular science titles, including several children's activity books. He works as a non-fiction editor, and lives with his wife and two children in Coon Rapids, Minnesota.

This is his first book of poetry.

For more, visit www.brettortler.com

About Fomite

A fomite is a medium capable of transmitting infectious organisms from one individual to another.

"The activity of art is based on the capacity of people to be infected by the feelings of others." Tolstoy, *What Is Art?*

Writing a review on Amazon, Good Reads, Shelfari, Library Thing or other social media sites for readers will help the progress of independent publishing. To submit a review, go to the book page on any of the sites and follow the links for reviews. Books from independent presses rely on reader to reader communications.

For more information or to order any of our books, visit http://www.fomitepress.com/FOMITE/Our_Books.html

More Titles from Fomite...

Novels
Joshua Amses — *During This, Our Nadir*
Joshua Amses — *Ghatsr*
Joshua Amses — *Raven or Crow*
Joshua Amses — *The Moment Before an Injury*
Jaysinh Birjepatel — *Nothing Beside Remains*
Jaysinh Birjepatel — *The Good Muslim of Jackson Heights*
David Brizer — *Victor Rand*
Paula Closson Buck — *Summer on the Cold War Planet*
Dan Chodorkoff — *Loisaida*
David Adams Cleveland — *Time's Betrayal*
Jaimee Wriston Colbert — *Vanishing Acts*
Roger Coleman — *Skywreck Afternoons*
Marc Estrin — *Hyde*
Marc Estrin — *Kafka's Roach*
Marc Estrin — *Speckled Vanities*
Zdravka Evtimova — *In the Town of Joy and Peace*
Zdravka Evtimova — *Sinfonia Bulgarica*

Daniel Forbes — *Derail This Train Wreck*
Greg Guma — *Dons of Time*
Richard Hawley — *The Three Lives of Jonathan Force*
Lamar Herrin — *Father Figure*
Michael Horner — *Damage Control*
Ron Jacobs — *All the Sinners Saints*
Ron Jacobs — *Short Order Frame Up*
Ron Jacobs — *The Co-conspirator's Tale*
Scott Archer Jones — *And Throw Away the Skins*
Scott Archer Jones — *A Rising Tide of People Swept Away*
Julie Justicz — *Degrees of Difficulty*
Maggie Kast — *A Free Unsullied Land*
Darrell Kastin — *Shadowboxing with Bukowski*
Coleen Kearon — *#triggerwarning*
Coleen Kearon — *Feminist on Fire*
Jan English Leary — *Thicker Than Blood*
Diane Lefer — *Confessions of a Carnivore*
Rob Lenihan — *Born Speaking Lies*
Douglas Milliken — *Our Shadow's Voice*
Colin Mitchell — *Roadman*
Ilan Mochari — *Zinsky the Obscure*
Peter Nash — *Parsimony*
Peter Nash — *The Perfection of Things*
George Ovitt — *Stillpoint*
George Ovitt — *Tribunal*
Gregory Papadoyiannis — *The Baby Jazz*
Pelham — *The Walking Poor*
Andy Potok — *My Father's Keeper*
Frederick Ramey — *Comes A Time*
Joseph Rathgeber — *Mixedbloods*
Kathryn Roberts — *Companion Plants*
Robert Rosenberg — *Isles of the Blind*
Fred Russell — *Rafi's World*
Ron Savage — *Voyeur in Tangier*
David Schein — *The Adoption*
Lynn Sloan — *Principles of Navigation*
L.E. Smith — *The Consequence of Gesture*

L.E. Smith — *Travers' Inferno*
L.E. Smith — *Untimely RIPped*
Bob Sommer — *A Great Fullness*
Tom Walker — *A Day in the Life*
Susan V. Weiss — *My God, What Have We Done?*
Peter M. Wheelwright — *As It Is On Earth*
Suzie Wizowaty — *The Return of Jason Green*

Poetry
Anna Blackmer — *Hexagrams*
Antonello Borra — *Alfabestiario*
Antonello Borra — *AlphaBetaBestiaro*
Antonello Borra — *The Factory of Ideas*
L. Brown — *Loopholes*
Sue D. Burton — *Little Steel*
David Cavanagh — *Cycling in Plato's Cave*
James Connolly — *Picking Up the Bodies*
Greg Delanty — *Loosestrife*
Mason Drukman — *Drawing on Life*
J. C. Ellefson — *Foreign Tales of Exemplum and Woe*
Tina Escaja/Mark Eisner — *Caida Libre/Free Fall*
Anna Faktorovich — *Improvisational Arguments*
Barry Goldensohn — *Snake in the Spine, Wolf in the Heart*
Barry Goldensohn — *The Hundred Yard Dash Man*
Barry Goldensohn — *The Listener Aspires to the Condition of Music*
R. L. Green — *When You Remember Deir Yassin*
Gail Holst-Warhaft — *Lucky Country*
Raymond Luczak — *A Babble of Objects*
Kate Magill — *Roadworthy Creature, Roadworthy Craft*
Tony Magistrale — *Entanglements*
Gary Mesick — *General Discharge*
Andreas Nolte — *Mascha: The Poems of Mascha Kaléko*
Sherry Olson — *Four-Way Stop*
Brett Ortler — *Lessons of the Dead*
Aristea Papalexandrou/Philip Ramp — *Μας προσπερνά/It's Overtaking Us*
Janice Miller Potter — *Meanwell*
Janice Miller Potter — *Thoreau's Umbrella*

Philip Ramp — *The Melancholy of a Life as the Joy of Living It Slowly Chills*
Joseph D. Reich — *A Case Study of Werewolves*
Joseph D. Reich — *Connecting the Dots to Shangrila*
Joseph D. Reich — *The Derivation of Cowboys and Indians*
Joseph D. Reich — *The Hole That Runs Through Utopia*
Joseph D. Reich — *The Housing Market*
Kenneth Rosen and Richard Wilson — *Gomorrah*
Fred Rosenblum — *Vietnumb*
David Schein — *My Murder and Other Local News*
Harold Schweizer — *Miriam's Book*
Scott T. Starbuck and Guy Denning — *Carbonfish Blues*
Scott T. Starbuck — *Hawk on Wire*
Scott T. Starbuck — *Industrial Oz*
Seth Steinz r — *Among the Lost*
Seth Steinzor — *To Join the Lost*
Susan Thomas — *In the Sadness Museum*
Susan Thomas — *The Empty Notebook Interrogates Itself*
Paolo Valesio/Todd Portnowitz — *La Mezzanotte di Spoleto/Midnight in Spoleto*
Sharon Webster — *Everyone Lives Here*
Tony Whedon — *The Tres Riches Heures*
Tony Whedon — *The Falkland Quartet*
Claire Zoghb — *Dispatches from Everest*

Stories
Jay Boyer — *Flight*
L. M Brown — *Treading the Uneven Road*
Michael Cocchiarale — *Here Is Ware*
Michael Cocchiarale — *Still Time*
Neil Connelly — *In the Wake of Our Vows*
Catherine Zobal Dent — *Unfinished Stories of Girls*
Zdravka Evtimova — *Carts and Other Stories*
John Michael Flynn — *Off to the Next Wherever*
Derek Furr — *Semitones*
Derek Furr — *Suite for Three Voices*
Elizabeth Genovise — *Where There Are Two or More*
Andrei Guriuanu — *Body of Work*
Zeke Jarvis — *In A Family Way*

Arya Jenkins — *Blue Songs in an Open Key*
Jan English Leary — *Skating on the Vertical*
Marjorie Maddox — *What She Was Saying*
William Marquess — *Boom-shacka-lacka*
Gary Miller — *Museum of the Americas*
Jennifer Anne Moses — *Visiting Hours*
Martin Ott — *Interrogations*
Christopher Peterson — *Amoebic Simulacra*
Jack Pulaski — *Love's Labours*
Charles Rafferty — *Saturday Night at Magellan's*
Ron Savage — *What We Do For Love*
Fred Skolnik— *Americans and Other Stories*
Lynn Sloan — *This Far Is Not Far Enough*
L.E. Smith — *Views Cost Extra*
Caitlin Hamilton Summie — *To Lay To Rest Our Ghosts*
Susan Thomas — *Among Angelic Orders*
Tom Walker — *Signed Confessions*
Silas Dent Zobal — *The Inconvenience of the Wings*

Odd Birds
William Benton — *Eye Contact: Writing on Art*
Micheal Breiner — *the way none of this happened*
J. C. Ellefson — *Under the Influence: Shouting Out to Walt*
David Ross Gunn — *Cautionary Chronicles*
Andrei Guriuanu and Teknari — *The Darkest City*
Gail Holst-Warhaft — *The Fall of Athens*
Roger Lebovitz — *A Guide to the Western Slopes and the Outlying Area*
Roger Lebovitz — *Twenty-two Instructions for Near Survival*
dug Nap— *Artsy Fartsy*
Delia Bell Robinson — *A Shirtwaist Story*
Peter Schumann — *Belligerent & Not So Belligerent Slogans from the Possibilitarian Arsenal*
Peter Schumann — *Bread & Sentences*
Peter Schumann — *Charlotte Salomon*
Peter Schumann — *Faust 3*
Peter Schumann — *Planet Kasper, Volumes One and Two*
Peter Schumann — *We*

Plays
Stephen Goldberg — *Screwed and Other Plays*
Michele Markarian — *Unborn Children of America*

Essays
Robert Sommer — *Losing Francis: Essays on the Wars at Home*

www.ingramcontent.com/pod-product-compliance
Lightning Source LLC
Chambersburg PA
CBHW020126130526
44591CB00032B/540